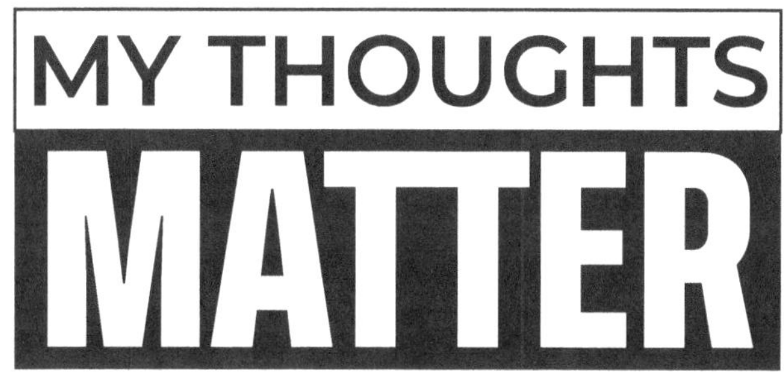

STRATEGIES FOR NAVIGATING INNER BLOCKS AND LIMITING BELIEFS

DR. ANGIE LESLIE

Table of Contents

Introduction:

The Concept of Limiting Beliefs

Limiting beliefs is when you do not pursue your dreams or passions to the fullest because you do not have enough faith in yourself that you can achieve them. To address these thoughts of limiting beliefs, you need to start by identifying and naming them. For example, a belief that "I'm not good enough" stemming from past failures, or "I don't deserve success" stemming from childhood experiences. To overcome these beliefs, you must first admit that they exist.

The purpose of this guide is to help you identify those limiting beliefs and the challenges that result from the limitations we place on ourselves. The goal is to be equipped with strategies that allow for overcoming these beliefs so we can live fulfilled lives.

One of the ways that we can counter-act these negative beliefs is by using affirmations — such as "I am capable of achieving my goals" — and visualization techniques to picture success.

This guide will help us identify some of the root causes of these limitations and examine some of their challenges, which will allow us to adopt a mindset change and develop positive thinking to cultivate a growth mindset.

Chapter 1

Understanding Limiting Beliefs

Navigating inner blocks and limiting beliefs can be challenging, but with the right strategies, you can work through them effectively. It is important that we understand how our belief system can hinder our growth and send us on a downward spiral. Achieving our full potential is conditioned upon a belief system that tells us that we can do it. If we have a belief system that says no, you can't, then guess what, you won't.

It is important to know that God has not placed any limitations on us, so why should we place them on ourselves? But unfortunately, we do. We have created our own glass ceiling, and once we reach it, we don't strive to go any further. As we press our way through life and work to get healed from certain setbacks resulting from life, we need to set our sights on breaking the glass ceiling and moving beyond self-imposed limitations.

Here are some approaches to consider:

1. Identify and Acknowledge

- Reflect on Your Beliefs: Take some time to pinpoint the limiting beliefs you hold. These might be about your abilities, worth, or potential. Journaling or meditation can help uncover these.

- Acknowledge Their Presence: Recognize that these beliefs are there and that they are influencing your actions and thoughts.

2. Challenge Your Beliefs

- Question Their Validity: Ask yourself if these beliefs are truly accurate. Are they based on evidence or assumptions?

- Seek Counterevidence: Look for examples from your own life or from others that contradict these limiting beliefs.

3. Reframe Your Perspective

- Change Your Narrative: Shift from a negative or limiting perspective to a more positive or empowering one. For instance, replace "I'm not good enough" with "I'm learning and growing every day."

- Visualize Success: Imagine yourself succeeding and achieving your goals. This can help in creating a more positive mindset.

4. Set Small, Achievable Goals

- Break Down Objectives: Start with small, manageable goals that align with your desired outcome. Achieving these can build confidence and momentum.
- Celebrate Small Wins: Recognize and reward yourself for each step you take toward overcoming your limiting beliefs.

5. Seek Feedback and Support

- Get a Different Perspective: Talk to trusted friends, mentors, or coaches who can provide an outside perspective and encouragement.
- Join Supportive Communities: Engage with groups or networks that can offer support and share experiences related to overcoming similar challenges.

6. Practice Self-Compassion

- Be Kind to Yourself: Understand that everyone has limiting beliefs and that it's a part of the human experience. Treat yourself with the same kindness and understanding you would offer a friend.
- Forgive Mistakes: Recognize that setbacks are part of the process, and don't let them derail your progress.

7. Engage in Continuous Learning

- Educate Yourself: Read books, take courses, or attend workshops related to personal development and mindset.
- Stay Curious: Cultivate a mindset of curiosity and growth rather than one of fixed limitations.

8. Use Affirmations and Visualization

- Affirm Positive Beliefs: Develop and repeat affirmations that support your new, empowering beliefs.
- Visualize Success: Regularly practice visualizing yourself achieving your goals, and overcoming obstacles.

9. Consider Professional Help: Therapy or Coaching: Sometimes, working with a therapist or coach can provide deeper insights and tools for overcoming deeply rooted limiting beliefs.

10. Be consistent: Keep Going: Changing limiting beliefs is a process that takes time. Be patient with yourself and stay committed to your growth journey.

Each person's path is unique, so it might be helpful to experiment with different strategies to see what resonates best with you.

Chapter 2

Uncovering the Roots of Limiting Beliefs

Fear and resistance are generally the root cause of most of the limitations we place on ourselves. More often than not, they arise from a desire to avoid discomfort or failure. They can manifest as procrastination, self-doubt, or avoidance behaviors. These feelings can be brought on by a variety of things, such as childhood trauma, feelings of abandonment, and rejection. When we begin to acknowledge the root cause, we can flip the switch to turn it from a negative experience to a positive experience. The idea here is to turn these into opportunities for growth.

Fear and resistance are natural responses, but acknowledging and addressing them is key to progress. Once we learn to accept these feelings without judgment and begin to understand their underlying causes, we can then use them as signals for areas needing growth. Techniques like journaling and seeking support can help in confronting these obstacles and moving forward with greater confidence.

A sound mind is crucial in addressing fear and resistance. Cultivating mental clarity and emotional resilience can make it easier to face challenges and navigate obstacles.

Here's how maintaining a sound mind can help:

1. **Self-Awareness**: A sound mind enhances self-awareness, enabling you to recognize when fear and resistance are influencing your thoughts and actions. This awareness is the first step in addressing these issues effectively.

2. **Emotional Regulation**: Practices like mindfulness and meditation help manage anxiety and stress, creating a more balanced emotional state. This stability can make fear and resistance less overwhelming.

3. **Critical Thinking**: A clear and focused mind can more objectively evaluate the validity of limiting beliefs and fears. This helps in challenging and reframing negative thoughts with rational and positive perspectives.

4. **Decision-Making**: A sound mind improves decision-making by allowing you to approach challenges with a calm and logical mindset rather than reacting out of fear or impulse.

5. **Resilience**: Developing mental resilience through techniques like cognitive-behavioral strategies and positive self-talk can strengthen your ability to confront and overcome resistance.

6. **Growth Mindset**: Embracing a growth mindset fosters an attitude of curiosity and learning, which helps in viewing challenges as opportunities rather than threats.

Things like journaling and self-reflection can help with your mental clarity. As a Christian, prayer and Bible study also helps with keeping your mind focused.

CASE STUDY:

The book *My Trauma Is Not My Story* chronicles the life of Adaeze as she dealt with the adverse effect that childhood trauma had on her life. It tells the story of the different phases of spiritual rebirthing she had to go through to arrive at the place of operating with a sound mind. Adaeze had to admit that the trauma was keeping her feeling bound and leaving her feeling alone and abandoned. The root of limiting beliefs was rooted in this trauma. She finally understood that she needed to move out of the place of just getting by into the place of abundance, which the Lord had spoken to us about. So, she adjusted her life, thoughts, and priorities to move into healing and fulfillment.

Adaeze's journey illustrates the importance of addressing and healing from trauma as a crucial step in finding one's life's purpose. She underscores the need to actively work through past difficulties and shift one's mindset towards resilience and positivity. Trusting in spiritual guidance or personal beliefs can provide direction and support during uncertain times. Adaeze also stresses that overcoming frustration and maintaining perseverance are essential for achieving one's dreams, even when confronted with significant challenges and limitations. Feel read to read *My Trauma Is Not My Story* to find out more about Adaeze.

Chapter 3

Breaking Through Limiting Beliefs

Breaking through limiting beliefs involves a combination of self-awareness, strategic action, and mental reprogramming. It is not something that happens overnight. It requires work and takes time. Persistence and consistency are the key. Breakthrough is something that you must go after. The enemy is not just going to let you have it. You must go after it with a newfound determination. That glass ceiling is hard to crack, so you must give it all you have in order to break it. The struggle will be real, but it also will be worth it.

Here are some detailed strategies to help you tackle and overcome these barriers:

1. Engage in Continuous Learning

- Read and Educate Yourself: Consume content related to personal development, psychology, and mindset. Books, articles, and courses can provide new perspectives and tools.

- Stay Curious: Cultivate a mindset of curiosity and openness to learning. This can help you approach challenges with a growth mindset rather than being constrained by limiting beliefs.

2. Practice New Behaviors

- Act: Act on the new beliefs you're developing. Taking concrete steps towards your goals can help solidify your new mindset.

- Experiment with New Approaches: Try new strategies or approaches to situations where you previously felt limited. This can help you discover new possibilities and reinforce your changing beliefs.

3. Monitor and Adjust

- Reflect Regularly: Periodically assess your beliefs and progress. Reflect on what's working and what might need adjustment.

- Be Flexible: Be willing to adjust your strategies as needed. Personal growth is an ongoing process, and flexibility can help you navigate it more effectively.

4. Consider Professional Guidance

- Therapy: If limiting beliefs are deeply ingrained or causing significant distress, working with a therapist can provide deeper insights and tailored strategies for change.
- Personal Development Coaching: A coach specializing in personal development can offer focused support and techniques to help you break through limiting beliefs.

By combining these strategies, you can create a comprehensive approach to overcoming limiting beliefs and achieving your personal and professional goals.

Chapter 4

Overcoming Self-Doubt and Negative Self-Talk

To overcome self-doubt and negative self-talk, start by identifying and challenging those thoughts. Those thoughts need to be replaced with positive affirmations. Learn to put more emphasis on your successes rather than your failures. Techniques like cognitive restructuring, where you reframe negative thoughts into constructive ones, can be effective. Daily practices such as journaling can also help build self-confidence and create a more supportive inner dialogue.

To replace negative thoughts, start with affirmations that reflect desired outcomes, such as "I am capable of achieving my goals." Pair these with constructive self-dialogue, where you focus on your strengths and past successes. Learn to be more intentional about reciting daily affirmations, participating in positive self-talk, and journaling to reinforce a more optimistic and supportive mindset.

A clear and focused mind allows you to recognize and challenge negative thoughts effectively. It supports the consistent practice of positive affirmations and constructive self-dialogue, making it easier to shift from self-doubt to confidence. Techniques like mindful reflection can help maintain mental clarity and support this transformative process.

DAILY AFFIRMATIONS

Affirmation:
I am capable of achieving my goals, no matter my age.
Proverb (Swahili):
"The best time to plant a tree was 20 years ago. The second best time is now."

Affirmation:
My past does not define my future; I embrace new opportunities.
Proverb (Chinese):
"A journey of a thousand miles begins with a single step."

Affirmation:
I release limiting beliefs and welcome growth with an open heart.
Proverb (Japanese):
"Fall seven times, stand up eight."

Affirmation:
I deserve happiness, success, and fulfillment.

Proverb " (Zulu):

"No matter how long the night, the day is sure to come."

Affirmation:

Each day, I am becoming a better version of myself.

Proverb (West African):

"Little by little, the bird builds its nest."

Affirmation:

My thoughts shape my reality, and today, I choose positive ones.

Proverb (Indian):

"All the flowers of all the tomorrows are in the seeds of today."

Affirmation:

I am resilient, strong, and confident in my abilities.

Proverb (Arabic):

"Sunshine all the time makes a desert."

Affirmation:

I let go of fear and embrace the unknown with courage.

Proverb (Latin):

"Fortune favors the brave."

Affirmation:

I am learning and growing every day; my journey is unique and valuable.

Proverb (Korean):

"Even if you know the way, ask one more time."

Affirmation:

I celebrate my small wins and honor my progress.

Affirmation:

I am not defined by my past mistakes but by the strength I show in moving forward.

Affirmation:

My inner wisdom guides me toward the best path for my life.

Affirmation:

I forgive myself and others, releasing all burdens and choosing peace.

Affirmation:

I am worthy of abundance, and I welcome it into my life with grace.

Affirmation:

I am enough just as I am, and I embrace my uniqueness.

Affirmation:

My mind is sound, my spirit is strong, and my heart is open to new possibilities.

Affirmation:

I trust the process of life and know that everything is unfolding as it should.

Chapter 5

Cultivating a Growth Mindset

Cultivating a growth mindset involves embracing the belief that abilities and intelligence can be developed through dedication and hard work. This mindset fosters resilience, motivation, and a love of learning. However, your mind must be ready for growth.

It is easy to say that we want to grow, but most people fail at it because they are not ready for what is required of them to grow. They are not ready to put in the work or the time to achieve their goals. We live in a world filled with shortcuts, which is the road that people what to take.

They don't want to take the long way. The Bible tells us that the race is not given to the swift but to those who endure to the end. You will need stamina to change. Even the shortcut can be long sometimes if you are not ready for change. Cultivating a growth mind means that you have made a conscious decision to tough it out, no matter how long it takes. Your heart, mind, body, and soul must all agree to see the full potential of a growth mindset.

1. Understanding the Growth Mindset

- Learn the Basics: Familiarize yourself with the concept of a growth mindset, popularized by psychologist Carol Dweck. Understand that it contrasts with a fixed mindset, which holds that abilities are static and unchangeable.

- Recognize the Benefits: Acknowledge how a growth mindset can positively impact various areas of your life, such as overcoming challenges, improving performance, and enhancing personal and professional relationships.

2. Embrace Challenges and Failures

- View Challenges as Opportunities: Approach challenges as chances to grow and learn. Instead of avoiding difficult tasks, tackle them with the mindset that you will gain valuable experience and skills.

- Learn from Failures: See failures as part of the learning process. Analyze what went wrong, extract lessons, and apply them to future endeavors. Adopt the belief that failure is not a reflection of your abilities but an opportunity to improve.

3. Cultivate a Love for Learning

- Set Learning Goals: Focus on setting goals related to learning and improvement rather than solely on outcomes. For example, aim to develop a new skill or deepen your understanding of a subject.

- Engage in Continuous Learning: Pursue opportunities for growth, such as taking courses, reading, or exploring new interests. Maintain a curious and open-minded approach to learning.

3. Develop Resilience and Perseverance

- Build Mental Resilience: Strengthen your ability to bounce back from setbacks. Practice self-compassion, stay positive, and use setbacks as motivation to persist.
- Practice Perseverance: Develop habits that promote persistence, such as setting incremental goals, celebrating small victories, and staying committed to your long-term objectives.

4. Surround Yourself with a Growth-Minded Community

- Engage with Like-Minded Individuals: Connect with people who have a growth mindset and share your values. Engage in discussions, collaborate on projects, and support each other's growth.
- Learn from Role Models: Identify role models who embody a growth mindset. Study their approaches, attitudes, and strategies for overcoming challenges and achieving success.

By implementing these strategies, you can effectively cultivate a growth mindset, leading to greater resilience, adaptability, and success in various aspects of your life.

Chapter 6

Integrating New Beliefs

Challenging and reframing beliefs that hold you back is a powerful way to shift your mindset and unlock your potential. This is what God is waiting for us to do: shift our mindset so that our will aligns with His will. Our thoughts dictate our actions. If our beliefs are limited, then our actions are limited. We will not be able to move fully into our purpose if our mind is telling us that we are trying to live out someone else's dreams. We must believe that the assignment is for us and start taking the necessary steps to bring forth manifestation.

Here is a step-by-step guide to help you with this process:

1. Reframe the Belief
- Create a New Perspective: Develop a positive and empowering alternative to your limiting belief. For instance, instead of "I'm not good enough," reframe it to "I have unique strengths and am continually improving."

- Use Affirmations: Craft affirmations that reflect your new belief. Repeat these daily to reinforce your new perspective. For example, "I am capable of achieving my goals and learning from challenges."

2. Test the New Belief

- Act: Put your new belief to the test by taking small, manageable steps that align with it. If your new belief is "I can lead effectively," take on a small leadership role or project to build confidence.
- Reflect on Results: Assess the outcomes of your actions. Positive results will help solidify the new belief, while any setbacks can be opportunities for further growth and adjustment.

3. Monitor Your Progress

- Keep a Journal: Document your experiences, feelings, and progress as you work on reframing your beliefs. This helps in tracking changes and recognizing patterns.
- Adjust as Needed: Be open to adjusting your new belief if you find that it needs refinement or if you uncover new insights.

4. Rejoice in the New Beliefs

- Celebrate Successes: Acknowledge and celebrate when you successfully act in alignment with your new beliefs. This reinforces the positive changes you're making.
- Continue Learning: Engage in ongoing personal development to keep your mindset growing and evolving.

This can include reading, attending workshops, or exploring new interests.

By following these steps, you can systematically challenge and reframe the limiting beliefs that held you back, paving the way for personal growth and achievement.

Adopting new perspectives that empower you can significantly enhance your personal growth and effectiveness.

Mental clarity is crucial in this process, as it helps you see things from a fresh angle and make informed decisions.

What beliefs do I need to change and why?

____

____

____

____

____

How do I plan to let go of these beliefs?

____

____

____

____

____

What are my new beliefs and habits?

____

____

____

____

____

What changes have I noticed about myself since changing old beliefs and establishing new beliefs and habits?

____

____

____

____

____

About the Author

Dr. Angie Leslie is the founder and CEO of Antioch-Global, a private non-profit Christian organization focused on discipleship training and leadership development as well as the founder and CEO of Dr. Angie Leslie Ministries and Spark Academy. The latter two of which is the basis for this work. She loves helping people achieve their goals and succeed in life. Success looks different for everyone, and Dr. Angie's call is to assist those assigned to me with defining what success looks like for them.

Achieving success means letting go of past hurts and failures to focus on your future. Having been a child of emotional abuse, she knows what it's like to feel lost, helpless, and alone. Experiencing any level of trauma is devasting to a person's ability to move forward because you are constantly reminded of the pain, but with God's help, all things are possible. Dr. Angie's role as a mentor is to create a safe place for people, mainly women, to be able to share and support each other as we all work to heal together. Through group mentoring sessions, we will learn to celebrate our wins and comfort each other through our losses.

Contact Information

Please be sure to check out our blog at sparkaca.org, where we celebrate each other's wins and comfort each other during times of loss.

Visit us at drangieleslie.com.com for other books by the author, including **My Trauma Is Not My Story** and for more details regarding our monthly group mentorship program: My Thoughts Matter.

You can also purchase the workbook **ABCs of Personal Fulfillment** to get on the road to personal fulfillment.